At Issue

| Beauty Pageants

Other Books in the At Issue Series:

At Issue

I Beauty Pageants

Tamara L. Roleff, Book Editor

GREENHAVEN PRESS
A part of Gale, Cengage Learning

GALE
CENGAGE Learning·

Farmington Hills, Mich • San Francisco • New York • Waterville, Maine
Meriden, Conn • Mason, Ohio • Chicago

Elizabeth Des Chenes, *Director, Content Strategy*
Cynthia Sanner, *Publisher*
Douglas Dentino, *Manager, New Product*

For more information, contact:
Greenhaven Press
27500 Drake Rd.
Farmington Hills, MI 48331-3535
Or you can visit our Internet site at gale.cengage.com

For product information and technology assistance, contact us at

Gale Customer Support, 1-800-877-4253
For permission to use material from this text or product, submit all requests online at www.cengage.com/permissions

Further permissions questions can be e-mailed to permissionrequest@cengage.com

Articles in Greenhaven Press anthologies are often edited for length to meet page requirements. In addition, original titles of these works are changed to clearly present the main thesis and to explicitly indicate the author's opinion. Every effort is made to ensure that Greenhaven Press accurately reflects the original intent of the authors. Every effort has been made to trace the owners of copyrighted material.

Cover image © Images.com/Corbis.

LIBRARY OF CONGRESS CATALOGING-IN-PUBLICATION DATA

Beauty pageants / Tamara L. Roleff, book editor.
    pages cm. -- (At issue)
    Includes bibliographical references and index.
    ISBN 978-0-7377-6824-4 (hardcover) -- ISBN 978-0-7377-6825-1 (pbk.)
    1. Beauty contests. I. Roleff, Tamara L., 1959- editor of compilation.
    HQ1219.B3497 2014
    791.6'6--dc23
                                                        2013038503

Printed in the United States of America
1 2 3 4 5 6 7 18 17 16 15 14

Contents

Introduction

The most well known of American beauty pageants is probably the Miss America pageant, which has been held since 1921. It started as a publicity stunt to draw crowds to Atlantic City, New Jersey, in the off-season, while it crowned the most beautiful single young woman in America. More than ninety years later, the Miss America Pageant has developed into a scholarship contest, and although it still judges women's beauty, it includes other components, such as a talent portion and an interview. Over the years, beauty pageants have evolved from being strictly for single young women to pageants for married women, women in wheelchairs, transgendered women, full-figured women, teens, men, and even toddlers.

Each age group has different types of pageants. Glitz pageants are the most elaborate and expensive—in terms of both time and money—of beauty pageants. The contestants in these types of events may spend thousands of dollars on costumes, entry fees, coaches, and other expenses. Hobby pageants are not quite as elaborate as glitz contests, requiring less time and financial investment from participants. Scholastic pageants focus less on beauty and glamour than glitz and hobby pageants, and they award scholarship money rather than prizes to the winner. And finally, natural pageants emphasize the natural beauty and character of contestants and generally attract participants who want to gain poise or confidence in public speaking.

The debut of the reality television show *Toddlers and Tiaras* on TLC in 2009 brought the behind-the-scenes world of glitz child pageants to the attention of American viewers. Many people were horrified by what they saw on the reality program. Some pageant mothers appeared to be forcing their young daughters to compete, and even leading them around on the stage during the competition. Some mothers became angry when their daughters did not perform well or did not win, and they took out their anger and frustration on the judges, other parents, and even the young girls.

In addition, the girls were made up to appear much older than their young ages. In glitz pageants, the contestants wear wigs, makeup, elaborate and costly outfits, and for the youngest girls, "flippers"—false front teeth to hide their baby or missing teeth. Some of their costumes outraged viewers, who claimed they sexualized the young girls. In a 2011 episode, four-year-old Maddy Verst was dressed in a Dolly Parton costume, complete with a padded bra and padded buttocks. New York-based clinical social worker Mark Sichel said the padding, wigs, flippers, and spray tans worn by the little contestants cause "the children tremendous confusion, wondering why they are not okay without those things." He added, "Little girls are supposed to play with dolls, not be dolls."[1] Melissa Henson, a spokeswoman for the Parents Television Council, called for TLC to cancel the show, saying, "This is the most blatant example of sexualization of a child that I have seen. . . . This has gone too far."[2]

Also in 2011, three-year-old Paisley Dickey wore a costume based on Julia Roberts's prostitute outfit in the 1990 movie *Pretty Woman*. Paisley strutted around the stage wearing a white tank top, blue miniskirt, black thigh-high boots, and a yellow wig. Sherri Shepherd, cohost of the daytime talk show *The View*, was aghast that Paisley's mother, Wendy Dickey, would dress her daughter in such a costume. "When are we going to stop sexualizing our children? Your job is to protect your child. . . . If you don't think pedophiles are watching this show, I have a bridge I want to sell you."[3] Tim Winter, president of the Parents Television Council, agreed that the pageants seem to be sexualizing young girls. "The entire premise of the show is troubling, is disturbing when you have the premise of the show is to sex up your little girl, but when you have them portraying the character of a prostitute . . .

you're taking away the youthful essence of these little girls. Three-year-old girls shouldn't be sexy."[4] A pageant mother on *Toddlers and Tiaras* was equally horrified. "Us pageant moms already take a huge rap for what we're doing with our little girls and it's outfits like that that give us a bad rap."[5]

However, the contestants' parents and others defend the reality show, the girls who compete, and the costumes the youngsters wear. Lindsay Jackson said she wore the same Dolly Parton outfit when she competed in pageants as a young girl and did not consider it outrageous when her daughter, Maddy Verst, wore it. "When she wears the fake boobs and the fake butt it's just an added extra bonus."[6] In fact, she said the judges loved it. "Everyone acts like I am trying to sexualize my daughter, but it's ridiculous. If I put Maddy in a Jason costume for Halloween, would people think I was trying to turn her into a serial killer?"[7] Paisley's mother Dickey also defended her daughter's *Pretty Woman* outfit. "We tend to score really well with it all the way around from most everybody."[8]

Parents and pageant supporters also argue that the pageants give the girls lots of good experiences. Katie Duff, who writes a blog about pageants, contends that pageants provide many positive aspects for the contestants. "Competing in pageants at a young age can instill strong self-confidence, self-esteem, and self-worth early on in a girl's life," she writes. There are other benefits as well, she asserts. Girls who compete develop a "go-getter spirit" and become "comfortable in front of large audiences and strangers."[9] Most girls compete in beauty pageants because they want to, not because their mothers are forcing them to compete. Another blogger, Helene Malmsio, notes that pageants can be very rewarding for young participants. "Pageants can be a wonderful experience for children. For one thing, they get comfortable being in front of crowds. . . . The kids play together backstage, and the parents often help each other. Some contestants have made lifelong friends at pageants."[10] In addition, supporters say the girls' dedication to competing in pageants can lead to dedication in other hobbies as well, such as music, theater, and dance, and to lifelong friendships with others who share their interests.

The arguments over whether beauty pageants objectify women and girls by emphasizing their physical appearance, or whether they give the contestants poise, confidence, and self-esteem, are among the issues covered in *At Issue: Beauty Pageants*. The contributors also debate the relevance of beauty pageants and whether transgendered women should be allowed to compete with "natural" women.

Notes

1. Quoted in Charlotte Triggs, "*Toddlers & Tiaras* Controversy: Are They Growing Up Too Fast?" *People*, September 14, 2011. www.people.com/people/article/0,,20527816,00.html.
2. Quoted in Charlotte Triggs, with Kay West and Elaine Aradillas, "Toddlers & Tiaras: Too Much Too Soon?" *People*, September 26, 2011. www.people.com/people/archive/article/0,,20531172,00.html.
3. Quoted in Andrea Canning and Jennifer Pereira, "Tot Dressed as Prostitute: 'Toddlers and Tiaras' Blasted for Airing Image of 3-Year-Old Pageant Contestant in Racy Costume," *Good Morning America*, September 12, 2011. http://abcnews.go.com/US/toddlers-tiaras-mom-defends-dressing-tot-prostitute-pageant/story?id=14497042.
4. *Ibid.*
5. *Ibid.*
6. *Ibid.*
7. Quoted in Charlotte Triggs, with Kay West and Elaine Aradillas, "Toddlers & Tiaras: Too Much Too Soon?" *People*, September 26, 2011. www.people.com/people/archive/article/0,,20531172,00.html.

8. Quoted in Mikaela Conley, "Pedophile's Delight? 'Toddlers and Tiaras' Star, 4, Dons Fake Boobs, Butt," *Good Morning America*, September 5, 2011. http://abcnews.go.com/Health /year-toddlers-tiaras-star-dons-fake boobs-butt/story?id =14430223.
9. Katie Duff, "The Pros & Cons of Beauty Pageants," *Twisted or Talented Toddlers in Tiaras*, November 5, 2011. http:// beautypagentsforchildren.blogspot.com/2011/11/pros -cons-of-beauty-pageants.html.
10. Helen Malmsio, "Child Beauty Pageants Pros and Cons," Squidoo.com, accessed October 13, 2013. www.squidoo .com/child-beauty-pageants-pros-and-cons.

1

Child Beauty Pageants Sexualize Young Girls

Karen Kataline

Karen Kataline, author of FATLASH! Food Police & the Fear of Thin, *is a writer, public speaker, and social worker who resides in Denver, Colorado.*

Parents who enter their children in beauty pageants often have an obsessive need to show off their daughters. They are trying to live vicariously through their children, a syndrome known as "Princess by Proxy." Young girls who are forced to perform in beauty pageants become sexualized at a young age and are not allowed to experience childhood.

I never thought it was terribly sinister that I was in beauty pageants as a kid. The problem wasn't so much the pageants themselves as the kind of parents who chose to put their children in them.

In my case, they were just part of my mother's obsessive need to show me off. She was a "stage mother on steroids" who first put me on the stage at the age of three, just as her mother had done with her. As part of her preoccupation with my weight and appearance, she policed what I ate and imposed severely restrictive diets.

A Darker Side

As a natural extrovert, I took to "show biz" rather well and received plenty of praise for my performances. But there was a darker side: The old men scratching their crotches while I performed in skimpy costumes. The latent and confusing fear of being looked at sexually, which continued even into adulthood. And the haunting sense that I had no face when it was not made up for the stage.

Though I was used to performing a lot as a child, I thought my mother was joking when she entered me in my first "Little Miss Pageant." Me? In a beauty pageant? I knew I could never be the delicate and demure girl in the framed photograph that was ever-present in our house. The blonde five-year-old in the picture was in a perpetual and perfect splits pose and adorned in a feathery, sequinned costume. My mother, circa 1931.

Martina Cartwright, PhD, RD, wrote the foreword for my book, *FATLASH! Food Police & the Fear of Thin—A Cautionary Tale* and has—at last—given us a name for the syndrome in which appearance-obsessed moms live vicariously through their children: "Princess by Proxy." That my mother was also a child performer is a particularly clear example of how generational and progressive the problem is. These "pageant parents" search for their lost childhoods through their children and, in so doing, rob the children of theirs.

Memories

I had no idea about the ways in which my early pageant experiences affected me until I was well into my thirties, when a flood of memories and feelings came back to me in vivid and sometimes frightening pictures.

> *I remembered that my tutu was so stiff I could rest my arms on it as I waited for my turn to perform. With bright red lips and bouncing, corkscrew curls I prepared to step out onto the stage as hundreds of people watched. Before I took my place in line, my mother bent down and looked me in the eye.*

> *"All right Susie Q, don't worry if you forget all the steps, just keep on shaking." Why did my Mother send me to dancing school if she didn't want me to do the steps? I asked myself. We*

made our entrance. As the other girls began our dance, I began to shake my hips—only a little at first, but by the end, I was shaking with all my might.

Mom rushed up to me when I finished. She was glowing. "You brought the house down!" she raved. "They ate you up!" I was near tears.

"But, Mommy, why did the people laugh at me?" my confused toddler self asked.

"They weren't laughing at you, Karen, they were laughing with you," she said. "You stole the show!" I swallowed my tears and studied my mother's face. I'd never seen her look so happy. I realized that I had done that. And I could do it again, too. All I had to do was keep on shaking.

Princess by Proxy was rarer when I experienced it in the 1960s. Today, the syndrome is on the brink of being accepted as part of popular culture.

I realised my mother exploited this for the show by directing me to shake my hips on purpose. It is also an example of how she sexualised me in ways I doubt the other mothers would ever have considered.

Rebellion

My mother's dietary restrictions continued to escalate until, at the age of seven, she put me on a five-hundred calorie a day diet. This fueled a rebellion in me, which grew into a weight problem that took years for me to understand. At sixteen, I weighed 285 pounds.

Despite the pain of my excess poundage, I achieved several unconscious secondary gains. My girth worked as protection. It was a *FATLASH*, if you will, against my mother's dietary controls and demands for thinness, as I tried to own my appetite. My weight created a much-needed boundary between her "self" and mine. It also guaranteed that there would never be another beauty pageant.

Princess by Proxy was rarer when I experienced it in the 1960s. Today, the syndrome is on the brink of being accepted as part of popular culture. I've grown up to see a collective repeat of many of the mistakes my mother made. *Toddlers and Tiaras* and "Honey Boo Boo" it's time to draw the line—with the power of education.

I tell my story as a cautionary tale and with the hope that we can spare yet another generation of girls from feeling the need to write a book like *FATLASH*. Child pageants will be an anathema when parents and audiences alike understand that boundaries are necessary for children to attain body ownership and a sense of body integrity. Sexualizing them rushes them past important developmental stages, and prevents them from reaching healthy adulthood. The greatest challenge for parents who live vicariously through their children may be to first recognize that they haven't successfully reached that level of adulthood themselves.

2

Children Compete in Beauty Pageants Because They Enjoy Them

Henry Meller

Henry Meller is a television producer and reporter working for Nine Network in Australia.

A young girl who is very successful in child beauty pageants enjoys participating in them because she wins, and she likes the money she receives as prizes. Her parents say their daughter would not enter the pageants if she did not enjoy them. People who believe that child beauty pageants sexualize young girls have a sick mind.

Most six-year-old girls spend their time playing with their dolls or watching The Wiggles. Eden Wood is not one of them. Her spare time is filled with hair appointments, fittings and spray tans.

Eden—the tiny darling of the controversial US child beauty pageant circuit—has no interest in being "normal". She wants to "be a superstar and rule the world".

[In August 2011], she kicks off her quest for world domination by heading Down Under to conquer Australia, a newcomer to child pageants. And far from retiring as some reports suggest, her agent says there's a new CD to promote and a film in the pipeline when she returns home.

Eden hails from Arkansas—a small town called Taylor, population 566. Arkansas is called "The Natural State", which is pretty funny given Eden's glammed-up appearance.

On the eve of her flight to Australia, *Woman's Day* meets the blonde mini-star at a pageant in Texas. She is caked in make-up with fluttering false eyelashes and an extravagant sequinned costume.

Eden may dream of being a superstar, but her mum is the driving force of the Eden Wood empire, with dolls, books, a record contract and an upcoming line of signature pageant dresses.

A Living Porcelain Doll

Dubbed the "new JonBenet Ramsey," Eden is strikingly similar to the child beauty pageant star who was found dead at her Colorado home in 1996. But Eden's made-up face and over-the-top outfits are a vision the fans who follow her career on the US reality TV show *Toddlers & Tiaras* have come to expect.

"She looks just like a porcelain doll," says Eden's mum Mickie, 46, a drama teacher who has been entering her daughter in competitions since she was a year old.

Eden's looks provoke love-hate responses. A storm of protests met the announcement that she would be travelling to Australia with the pageant company Universal Royalty.

Critics claimed pageants sexualised children, and Eden's family even received death threats. Many people allege the little girl's dance moves—such as stripping off her jacket and spanking her backside while performing her song *Squirrels In My Pants*—are questionable, but Mickie won't hear of it and staunchly rebuts such criticisms.

"She's only doing that because the song is called *Squirrels In My Pants*," she says. "If you see sex when you look at my six-year-old child, that's not her fault and it's not my fault. It's just a sign of somebody being sick in the mind."

Eden's Mom a Driving Force

Child beauty pageants may divide opinion, but one thing not up for debate is Eden's personality. Whether being crowned with a sparkly tiara or trying to catch frogs in the mud on the family farm, she's polite and bubbly. Mickie has worked hard to ensure her little girl is well behaved and is determined that she "doesn't turn out another Lindsay Lohan."

"The closest thing to what I want for Eden would probably be Miley Cyrus but even she has gone off the rails," Mickie says.

Eden may dream of being a superstar, but her mum is the driving force of the Eden Wood empire, with dolls, books, a record contract and an upcoming line of signature pageant dresses.

Mickie regularly drives Eden eight hours to pageants, and has spent more than $100,000 on costumes—including more than $4000 for a single contest outfit that transformed her daughter into a Las Vegas showgirl.

She denies she planned to turn Eden into a star from the moment she was born.

"She started pageants when she was 14 months old," Mickie says. "I'd heard about a pageant a few days beforehand. When we got there, there were all these babies and little girls in the most incredible dresses, and that's when I started to see how pageants worked."

No Extreme Makeovers

Mickie maintains she would never inflict any extreme makeovers on her daughter.

"The Botox mum [San Francisco's Kerry Campbell, who said she injected her eight-year-old daughter Britney with Botox, then refuted the claims] is crazy," she says. "Why would anyone want to inject poison into their baby?" Botox isn't the only line Mickie won't cross. She is also opposed to waxing.

"I have heard of some mums taking their girls for 'virgin waxing'—where they wax the girls' bikini area so they never grow pubic hair.

I would never do that with Eden. No way!" Eden's eyebrows do, however, get shaved. "It's so gentle she can't even feel it," Mickie says. In her first pageant, Eden won the title of "prettiest hair". A few weeks later, Mickie entered her in another one. "I took her in her best Sunday dress and she won the whole darn thing! Ever since then, we've been on a roll."

Eden's dad, Louis, is clearly proud of his daughter's achievements too.

"As long as she keeps enjoying it, that's all that matters," he says. "It might not have been a very good idea if she wasn't pretty—but she is and I'm proud of what she's done."

Winning

How much Eden would enjoy pageants if she weren't so successful is probably answered when she's asked what she likes most about them. "Winning," she says. Why? "Because I like getting money."

She's spent some of her winnings on "dolls and lots of other dolls," as well as "a chihuahua called Bell BabyCakes."

Her earnings are set to skyrocket too. She's just performed around the US in a show called *The Glamour Girls Tour, Starring Eden Wood*, with two other pageant princesses.

"It's a chance for Eden to move on from pageants, to do her songs," Mickie says.

"I don't want to say the other girls are just filler—but they are there to give Eden some time between her performances."

No Regrets

Things are set to ramp up even more, with a new CD called *Cutie Patootie*, a role in an animated film and an audition for a feature film. Her mum is giving up her job so she can provide maximum support for Eden's full-scale push to become an international superstar.

"We wouldn't have to move to Hollywood full time, we'd always keep the farm," she says. "But you don't want her to look back and think what could have been for her if we had given her the chance."

For the moment, Eden is excited about visiting Australia and knows exactly what she wants to do while she's here.

"I wanna ride a kangaroo!" she shouts, hopping along with her ringlets bouncing. This may not be possible, but you get the feeling that where Eden Wood is concerned, just about anything else might be.

3

Child Beauty Pageants Give Children Unrealistic Expectations

Martina M. Cartwright

Martina M. Cartwright is a registered dietitian who holds a PhD in nutritional science and biomolecular chemistry. She has studied child beauty pageants and published her findings in the article "Princess by Proxy" in the November 2012 Journal of the American Academy of Child and Adolescent Psychiatry.

Activities such as beauty pageants that focus on physical appearance at an early age can have a detrimental effect on a child's self-esteem, body image, and self-worth later in life. These children may struggle with ideas of perfection, eating disorders, and body image in their adulthood. Pageants send a message that looks and appearance are more important than brains and education. Performing in beauty pageants can be a wonderful experience for children if their parents ensure that they participate in other activities that don't involve fancy costumes, makeup, and the world of make-believe.

The recent issue of *French Vogue* [August 2011] has sparked outrage for its photos of a ten-year old model lying in a sea animal print wearing a chest revealing gold dress, stilettos and heavy make up. Cries of "how young is too young" to model, be "sexy" etc. have ignited controversy about early sexualization of children. However, what of the looming concern of programming young children to be ultra conscious about physical appearance and the impact on adult body image and disordered eating?

A Billion Dollar Industry

Today, television is peppered with reality shows that feature pint-sized beauty queens decked out in pricy gowns, full make up and big hair. Pageants aren't the "dress up" play we knew as little girls, they are a multimillion-dollar industry. And it's not just beauty pageants. A recent reality dance program showed 9-year-olds prancing around in revealing two-piece costumes complemented by thigh high stockings, spackled make up and teased hair. Before hitting the stage the choreographer demanded that they "paint on abs." Armed with spray bronzer, the moms dutifully "carved" abs into their daughter's bare midriffs just before the young girls performed a provocative dance that cause audible gasps from the audience.

Many experts agree that participation in activities that focus on physical appearance at an early age can influence teen and/or adult self-esteem, body image and self-worth. Issues with self-identity after a child "retires" from the pageant scene in her teens are not uncommon. Struggles with perfection, dieting, eating disorders and body image can take their toll in adulthood.

Child performers may believe that parental and/or adult love or approval are anchored to how perfectly they look or how well they ignite the stage with their presence.

"The Princess Syndrome"

Not all pageant participants, young dancers or performers will have body issues when they get older, but some do. For the girls who do develop image obsessions, it appears that the hypercritical environment of their youth produces a drive towards the unattainable goal of physical perfection. "The Princess Syndrome" as I like to call it, is a fairy tale. Unrealistic expectations to be thin, physically beautiful, and perfect are at the heart of some disordered eating behaviors and body dissatisfaction. Scant research has been conducted to see if former pint-sized beauty pageant participants are more likely to suffer from eating disorders, but a small study published in 2005 showed that former childhood beauty pageant contestants had higher rates of body dissatisfaction.

In my experience as a dietitian for high-powered entertainment groups, I found that many of the young women with eating disorders were trained at an early age to value physical perfection, thinness, athletic prowess and attractiveness. When it comes to performing, education takes a backseat. The performer's bodies are their livelihood and less-than-perfect might lead to unemployment. Granted, practice and devotion are required to hone any skill, but when does dedication go to far?

The child pageant and dance circuits are competitive, demanding and stressful. Watch any reality dance or pageant show and see how children are placed under enormous pressure to perform flawlessly. Tears, tantrums and fits frequently ensue with some adults mocking crying children. As result, child performers may believe that parental and/or adult love or approval are anchored to how perfectly they look or how well they ignite the stage with their presence. Long practice sessions are the norm and interfere with social activities, sleep and homework. Just the other day, a popular dance show featured adults candidly admitting that they encourage activity over education. When confronted, devotees said, "My daughter loves it." Or "Ask her if she likes doing it!" Money, ratings and attention fuel the pageant/dance media machine with parents and adults reaping the benefits.

Long-Term Impact on Girls

Adults need to be aware of the potential long-term impact super-competitive, beauty-driven pursuits can have on a young girl's psyche. Intense participation in activities that spotlight physical appearance instills the idea that physical beauty and superficial charm are the keys to success, thus making self-worth and self-esteem inextricably tied to attractiveness. The take home message for society is that natural beauty or brains aren't enough to "make it." Case in point: At a local "Women in Business" mixer I joined a circle of attractive 50-somethings who were discussing a local child pageant. All were lamenting the "work that goes in to being beautiful and successful." Being new to the group, they asked what I did for a living, when I told them I was a scientist I was met with "Oh, you must be smart." In many social circles, looks and appearance trump brains and education. My response: "Looks are fleeting, brains are forever."

Youthful participation in pageants and dance competitions can be a wonderful experience and may lead to a rewarding career. The key is to provide performing children with a balance of activities that involve more than fancy costumes, make-up and the world of make-believe. The feeling of unconditional love from a parent or nurturing adult can do wonders to curb body dissatisfaction, poor self-esteem and body image distress. As an example, a few years ago one of my clients had a dance career cut short by an injury. She said she was one of the few childhood dancers in her peer group that didn't have an eating disorder. We discussed what made her unlike most of her dancing cohorts and she summed it up like this, "Thankfully my mom made me study in between dance competitions. Dance was important, but so were school and friends. I went to college on a dance scholarship but minored in business. I can get a job that doesn't depend on my dance prowess or my looks and that fills me with confidence;

some of my friends judge themselves based on their looks or dance ability and they can never be perfect enough especially when it comes to diet."

Pretense

Not all tender-aged models, dancers, entertainers or pageant contestants will be offered a balanced childhood filled with unconditional love. For these kids, the constant "play acting" may create hyper-competitive, shallow adults who are never satisfied; perhaps making them think [in the words of singer Jim Morrison from The Doors], "Most people love you for who you pretend to be. To keep their love, you keep pretending—performing. You get to love your pretence. It's true, we're locked in an image, an act."

4

Beauty Pageants Build Confidence and Poise

Becca Horton

Becca Horton was a student majoring in communications at Mississippi State University at the time she wrote this viewpoint.

Beauty and scholarship pageants have awarded millions of dollars to women and girls of all ages to help them become leaders of tomorrow. While the contestants' appearance is important, so are other aspects, such as their personality and achievements. Pageants help women develop confidence and poise. Many women who compete in pageants go on to have successful careers.

Once upon a time, there was a beautiful girl from Gering, Nebraska. She hoped to become a lawyer one day, maybe a judge and then some sort of politician. But she gave all that up for a while and worked for a very different goal.

She strutted herself in a black bikini as well as a white evening gown, played "White Water Chopsticks" on the piano for a panel of judges and voiced her issues on website security. And the next thing she knew, Teresa Scanlan was Miss America 2011.

We all know stereotypes follow pageant contestants around like a shadow, inescapable no matter what light the girl stands in. Contestants are known sometimes for answering questions with answers that sometimes are completely inappropriate or, in other words, dumb. But before we are too judgmental toward the contestants, do we even know much about the pageants themselves?

Different Types of Pageants

There are six pageants we have all probably heard of: Miss America, Miss Universe, Miss USA, Miss World, Miss Teen USA, and Outstanding Teen. There are also multiple types of pageants: full-glitz pageants, natural pageants, semi-glitz pageants, face pageants, scholarship pageants, co-ed pageants, online pageants and online photo shoots.

The Miss America pageant was recently aired on ABC in January 2011, crowning the Nebraska contestant a winner for the first time in its 90-year history.

Pageants have always been plagued with controversy, ever since 6-year-old pageant cutie JonBenet Ramsey was murdered on Christmas Eve in her parent's home back in 1996.

There were pictures of her wearing provocative outfits and making her an object of inappropriate sexual fantasies that were scrutinized heavily by the press.

Since this tragedy, child pageants have been under heavy scrutiny. Some claim beauty pageants are more for the parents than for the children.

Pageants help the women learn confidence, poise and sometimes give them an opportunity to make friends for life.

Dismantling the Stereotypes

But the purpose of this article is to shed the stereotypes I once believed in like a child believes in Santa Claus.

I recently shed my opinions after a girl from my high school, who was this year in my public speaking class, gave a speech about the importance of pageants and their purpose of shaping America's young women.

I had never really talked to her in high school; we just passed each other in the hallways. But I had always known she was hardcore into the beauty pageant scene, and from what I'd heard, she was good at it, too.

The Leaders of Tomorrow

When she gave her speech that day, I made sure to pay attention. The Miss American Coed Pageants have awarded more than $12 million in scholarships and awards to women of many ages with qualities that help them become "the leaders of tomorrow."

Pageants help the women learn confidence, poise and sometimes give them an opportunity to make friends for life. According to the pageant center website, contestants' appearance is important, but no more so than their unique personality, ability to get along with others and their achievements.

It's true that pageant contestants have made IQ errors in the past, but not all of them can be judged for this mistake.

We need to get it through our heads that this scholarship opportunity is a character-building experience, and these contestants may end up being our lawyers. They may end up being our judges. And they may end up being our politicians. Despite certain beliefs, I have recently come to feel that pageants are not at all a joke; pageants are very serious for some.

We put all of our efforts into our sports, into our studies, into our video games. The only things these girls do differently is work hard for their image.

5

Beauty Pageants Are Not Appropriate for Young Children

Vernon R. Wiehe

Vernon R. Wiehe is professor emeritus in the University of Kentucky College of Social Work. He is the author of numerous books and professional articles and has lectured extensively on the subject of family violence, including child abuse.

Participating in beauty pageants is generally not an age-appropriate activity for young children but is often forced on them by their parents. Beauty pageants are significantly different from "dress-up." Young girls who participate in pageants become sexualized by wearing adult style clothing, makeup, and assuming provocative poses. Parents who force their children to participate in beauty pageants can be emotionally and physically abusive. Children who participate in beauty pageants also miss out on playing, which is an important part of childhood development.

*T*oddlers and Tiaras is a televised beauty pageant for very young children which appears weekly ironically on The Learning Channel. The Web site for the show describes it this way: "On any given weekend, on stages across the country, little girls and boys parade around wearing makeup, false eyelashes, spray tans and fake hair to be judged on their beauty, personality, and costumes. *Toddlers and Tiaras* follows families on their quest for sparkly crowns, big titles and lots of cash."

A TV viewer will see the program's feeble attempts at Las Vegas-like glamour and glitz in a rented hotel ballroom or school auditorium with primarily little girls in adult-like pageant attire parading in front of a small audience consisting largely of participants' families. The tots' attire includes makeup, hair extensions and "flippers" to hide missing teeth. Mothers, often overweight, engage in silly antics coaching the children in every move of their routines with the hope of winning a trophy taller than the child, a rhinestone crown, the title of "Ultimate Grand Supreme" and possibly some cash.

The viewer will also be taken behind the scenes to witness temper tantrums from children resisting the role into which they are being put. On a recent show, a 2-year-old cried the entire time on stage; in another show, a mother literally dragged the child around the stage supposedly putting the child through her routine.

Are Pageants for the Child or the Adult?

It raises questions for the viewer: Whose idea is this—the child's or the adult's? Is participating in such pageants age-appropriate behavior for a small child? Might such participation even represent a potential danger for the child's emotional development?

The potential impact of child beauty pageants may be viewed in terms of the fallacious arguments most frequently cited in support of this activity:

Playing Dress-up

All little girls like to play dress up at some time.

Dress-up, a sign of a child identifying with or mimicking the mother, is significantly different from organized child beauty pageants.

First, dress-up play generally is an activity engaged in by a young girl alone or with a group of playmates at home rather than on a stage in front of an audience.

Second, competition, an important element in child beauty pageants, ranks contestants, with one child becoming a winner and the others losers.

One of the most dangerous aspects of these pageants is the sexualization of young girls.

Third, dress-up involves little girls wearing their mothers' cast-off clothing or cosmetics in a way the child perceives mother uses these objects. Participants in *Toddlers and Tiaras* spend hundreds and even thousands of dollars for costumes, cosmetics and even beauty consultants.

Parents certainly have a right to spend their money on children as they wish, but if this expenditure of money and effort is for the ultimate goal of the child winning the contest and the child fails to do so, what is the emotional cost to the child? What happens to the child's self-esteem?

Sexualization of Young Girls

Children's beauty pageants teach poise and self-confidence.

Even if the pageants do foster the development of these attributes, the question must be raised whether poise and self-confidence stemming from beauty pageants is age appropriate for the child. One of the most dangerous aspects of these pageants is the sexualization of young girls.

Sexualization occurs through little girls wearing adult women's clothing in diminutive sizes, the use of makeup which often is applied by makeup consultants, spray tanning the body, the dying of hair and the use of hair extensions, and assuming provocative postures more appropriate for adult models.

The sexualization of young children sends a conflicting message to the child and a dangerous message to adults. To the child, a message is given that sexuality—expressed in clothing, makeup and certain postures—is appropriate and even something to exploit. The message to adults, especially pedophiles, is one condoning children as sexual objects. Research on child sexual abuse shows that the sexualization of children is a contributing factor to their sexual abuse.

Children Are Eager to Please Adults

Children enjoy participating in beauty pageants.

While young children may express enjoyment in participating in pageants, children are eager to please adults. Sleeping with their hair in curlers, having to sit quietly while their hair is being tinted or rolled, fake nails being applied or their body being spray tanned hardly seems like activities very young girls would choose over having fun with friends in age-appropriate play. The negative reactions of many of the participants in *Toddlers and Tiaras* testify to this.

Child Abuse?

Participation in beauty pageants is no different from participating in athletic or Suzuki music education programs.

Children's athletic programs and music education programs teach skills appropriate to the developmental stage of the child upon which the child can build later in life rather than emphasizing the beauty of the human body that can change significantly with time. In Suzuki recitals, for example, the unique contribution of each child is recognized and no child loses.

Do child beauty pageants constitute child abuse?

This question must be answered on an individual basis. Parents who force their children to participate in pageants, as well as in athletic and music education programs, can be emotionally and even physically abusive, if participation is meeting parental needs rather than the needs of the child.

The risk for such abuse to occur is perhaps greatest when children are not recognized for what they are—children—but rather are forced to assume miniature adult roles.

Play is an important factor in children's early development because, through play, they learn skills for adulthood.

After all, what is the rush to become an adult?

6

Beauty Pageants Are Irrelevant

Jose Flores

Jose Flores is a contributing writer for Starpulse.com, a leading entertainment news media organization.

Americans have paid little attention to beauty pageants for several decades. The fact that a woman of Lebanese heritage won the Miss USA beauty pageant in 2010 does not indicate that race relations are improving, nor is it a sign that Muslims are infiltrating US society or of a terrorist victory, as some conservative pundits claim. The media attention surrounding the crowning of a woman of Lebanese descent has more to do with the controversial questions asked by the judges—and intentionally inserted by the pageant owner Donald Trump—than by the ethnic heritage of its winner.

B eauty pageants are irrelevant.

   Short of Donald Trump, I don't think anybody knew the Miss USA pageant was happening, and short of the judges and contestants, I don't think anybody cared that Rima Fakih took home the crown. This was as big a non-story as could be, just an attractive girl winning an obsolete contest and getting a purely symbolic title. How nice for her. Let's move on. But Rima Fakih is not just an attractive girl who won an American beauty pageant; Rima Fakih is an attractive *Lebanese-*

American girl who won an American beauty pageant, which somehow means that Miss USA now becomes an acceptable litmus test with which to gauge the political climate of our country.

A Sign of an Ideological Shift

The left will celebrate this as proof that America will no longer stand for intolerance and oppression. They will get up on rooftops shouting about black presidents and middle-eastern beauty queens, and though I'm not sure that this is an altogether logical response, it is at the very least rooted in some sort of fact. Certainly, recent events have shown that our society is moving closer and closer to that idealized place where people are judged only by their character and ability, and not by their skin color and heritage. Rima Fakih's pageant victory is certainly a sign of this ideological shift. That said, this is a single victory in a beauty pageant that hasn't mattered since the 1980s, so I don't think anyone should be getting too giddy.

Similarly, there's no reason for the right wing to lose its mind like it has in the wake of Rima Fakih's Miss USA victory. The conservative response ranges from the illogical (blaming affirmative action) to the disgusting (calling Rima Fakih a terrorist), and has done nothing but bring publicity to an event which would have otherwise gone from irrelevant to forgotten in a matter of days. Just like winning the Miss USA pageant isn't a shining beacon of improved race relations, it certainly isn't a sign of Muslim infiltration or terrorist victory. If the terrorists plan to destroy America by planting a sleeper Miss USA, then they're far dumber than we could have imagined and we have absolutely nothing to worry about.

A Conspiracy?

Of course, none of the this controversy would have ever gotten off the ground if Rima Fakih hadn't stumbled in her evening gown, or if those stripper pole pictures had never been released, or if runner-up Miss Oklahoma hadn't been asked a question about the Arizona immigration law. Doesn't this conflagration of events prove that there's some sort of conspiracy to give Rima Fakih the crown?

No.

For starters, the stripper pole pictures. I see a fully-clothed adult woman doing a dance (albeit a provocative one) as part of a radio promotion. I don't see anything offensive or immoral about it. I've seen Miley Cyrus, Lindsay Lohan, and other so-called "child" stars do far worse. Let's move on.

The same goes for the evening gown stumble. People trip sometimes. Maybe we should be praising the pageant judges for recognizing that poise is not something that makes you perfect, but rather something that allows you to recover from moments of imperfection. I'd take a confident woman who can stumble and recover over a Stepford Wife any day.

The Interview Questions

Let's move on, then, to the questions that seem to have gotten everyone riled up. Rima Fakih was asked if she believed birth control should be covered by health insurance, and she replied affirmatively while calling birth control a "controlled substance." The critics pounced on Fakih's supposed ignorance, but was her answer really all that wrong? Obviously, birth control is not a controlled substance, but haven't we all made ourselves look foolish at one point or another by using technical terms we don't fully understand? And what's so wrong about suggesting that medical insurance should cover birth control? Though it isn't a medical necessity, it could certainly be considered preventative in the same way that annual check-ups or eye exams are. These things are not technically necessary, but they are in place to prevent necessary (and far more expensive) procedures down the line. It's not a cut and dry example, but the argument can certainly be made.

So what about the other incendiary question, the one that supposedly lost Miss Oklahoma the crown? She was asked if Arizona's newly passed immigration law strayed into territory that the federal government should be regulating, and in her response expressed support for states' rights, Arizona's in particular. Critics claim that she was penalized for not denouncing the Arizona immigration law, and this may very well be true. But what exactly is the problem if it is? We all know that sticking to a principle can have negative consequences. If Miss Oklahoma does not think that Arizona's immigration law deserves condemnation, then she should be praised for sticking to her beliefs. However, she must have known the possible consequences of answering that question as she did. As much as these girls prepare, she must have known who the judges were, and where their sensibilities lay. In other words, Miss Oklahoma knew she was taking a risk when she answered the question. She gambled, and unfortunately for her, she lost.

Rima Fakih winning was the icing on the cake, but her victory wasn't predetermined because of her heritage.

Breathing New Life Into a Dead Pageant

So now Rima Fakih is Miss USA. Half the country's outraged, half is elated, and watching from one of his many penthouses, Donald Trump is the most excited of them all. He knows there is only one conspiracy here, and he knows it is of his own creation. It's no coincidence that the same pageant that gave us a gay marriage question in 2009 has followed up with an illegal immigration question in 2010. Donald Trump knows how to get attention, and he's found a way to breathe new life into a pageant that's been dead for 20 years.

Rima Fakih winning was the icing on the cake, but her victory wasn't predetermined because of her heritage. Let's not forget that last year's gay marriage controversy kept the pageant in the news even though the winner and the runner-up were both white blondes. There is a bit of a conspiracy at play, but it begins and ends with Donald Trump and the questions he wants asked. Beyond that, he doesn't care who takes the crown, because he knows the real winner is his pageant, which has suddenly become newsworthy again.

7

Beauty Pageant Contestants Require Training and Coaching Like Athletes

John Przybys

John Przybys is a reporter for the Las Vegas Review-Journal.

Pageant coaches offer contestants advice on hair, wardrobe, and makeup, as well as choreography, interviewing skills, and other important aspects of beauty contests. Just as professional athletes need coaches to help them improve their skills, so, too, do pageant contestants. These participants are often able to take the skills they've learned for pageants and apply them to real-life situations, such as job interviews and school activities.

Elizabeth Mueller is a 5-year-old ball of barely contained energy wrapped up in a bubblegum-colored dress.

Whether she's strutting across the rehearsal room floor to a rock 'n' roll number or ambling and sashaying to a country beat, Elizabeth demands the attention of everyone in the room.

Seriously, she does. Prefacing her rendition of "The Star-Spangled Banner" with an invitation to an imaginary audience to stand, she points to a crouching photographer and says sternly, "I include you, Mr. Cameraman."

Credit Elizabeth's effervescent personality to, perhaps, a cosmic luck of the draw. But for her confidence and ability to feel comfortable performing in front of total strangers, offer props to Georgina Vaughan, Elizabeth's pageant coach.

Give Vaughan credit, also, for Elizabeth's enviable pageant record. She has competed in nearly 20 pageants since Vaughan became her coach about a year ago, and has won all but one (and that, Vaughan recalls, laughing, was only because Elizabeth was so busy playing to the stage-side photographer that "she wouldn't get off the stage").

For Elizabeth, competing in pageants—and doing all of the dancing, singing and performing that entails—is just something that she loves to do. But, even if she doesn't realize it, Elizabeth, with Vaughan's help, also is learning skills and developing confidence that will serve her well throughout life.

If anybody knows about the benefits of pageantry, it's Vaughan, whose roster of pageant titles includes reigns as Miss Nevada Teen USA 2006 and Miss Nevada USA 2009. Now, as owner of Winning Wand Pageant Consulting, Vaughan passes on the skills she has learned to other pageant hopefuls.

Pageant Coach

As a pageant coach, Vaughan offers clients—women and also, she notes, one man at present—advice on hair, wardrobe and makeup. She does choreography and photography. And, she offers clients strategies to effectively handle interview questions and other vital aspects of pageant competition that casual viewers may miss.

"When I tell people what my job is, they look at me kind of cross-eyed: 'You make a living at that?'" Vaughan says. "And I explain that, even when I was Miss Nevada, it's not just, 'Eat healthy and go on stage and just look pretty.' It's so much more than that."

Vaughan, 23, estimates that, since creating Winning Wand just more than a year ago, she has worked with more than 50 clients in Nevada, California and Arizona.

"Honestly, it was just going to be a hobby, then, all of a sudden, it just took off," she says. "There was such a demand from kids and adults wanting coaching. I've literally coached somebody as young as 2 years old to someone who's 40."

Different Approaches

Working with very young kids does require a different approach from working with teens or young women, Vaughan says. For a 2-year-old, for instance, the focus will be mostly on having fun, although young kids also can develop such skills as being comfortable in front of crowds.

You can see a difference with the girls on stage as to those who have some training and coaching and those who do not.

Vaughan says she sometimes suggests to parents that they return with their children when the kids are more ready to benefit from pageant training.

Brittney Cobb, 27, started competing in pageants at the age of 5. Three years ago, she created Fit for the Crown, her own Las Vegas pageant consulting firm.

Just Like Any Other Sport

"I tell people that (pageantry is) just like anything that you'd compete in in life," Cobb says. "There are professional football players who get paid millions of dollars, yet they still have coaches and they still need to train and work to perform their best.

"It's the same with pageantry, and you can see a difference with the girls on stage as to those who have some training and coaching and those who do not."

Cobb so far has worked with more than 60 clients ranging in age from 4 to 65, and says her philosophy is to "polish and bring out the best qualities and best features" of each.

"There are some very basic guidelines and, kind of, tricks of the trade," she says. "But, all in all, it's just about helping the individual's personality come through, and shine and capture the judges' attention."

Like any other sport or activity, pageantry requires that competitors learn skills from trained coaches.

Skills Translate Well Off Stage

Vaughan notes that the skills pageant contestants work to develop—confidence, poise and the ability to interact with others, speak to a crowd, think on your feet and excel in an interview—translate well to job searches, school, careers and life off of the stage.

"I've had people say, 'Can you just spend time with my daughter?' because you're a role model and, in the teenage years, they're not listening to parents," she says. "I can do that. Sometimes it feels like a psychology session."

Pageant training largely is about becoming "comfortable in your own skin," Vaughan adds. Toward that end, she promotes pageants "that have interviews in them, because—no joke— when I was growing up, because of all the (pageant) interviews I had been in, I have never not gotten a job, because I was so used to telling people, 'This is what I have to offer.'"

Cobb agrees, saying, "For me, it's all about building people's self-confidence.

"I had one young lady I worked with, and her teacher the following year told her mom, 'Wow, she's the best speaker in class.' She would just get up to do a book report or whatever, and she did such a great job, and her mom kind of credited (her) working with me as giving her the confidence to do that."

Cathy Kennedy's daughter, Marilyn, 14, has been competing in pageants since age 7 and now works with Vaughan.

"I've been to a couple of different coaches and Georgina is the best," Kennedy says. "She's reliable and she's honest, and that's very important with kids."

Not Any More Expensive

Pageant coaches don't work for free—Vaughan's basic fee, for example, is $50 per hour—but Kennedy notes that pageantry is "just like any other sport" that a child might participate in.

"I don't think it's any more expensive than any other sport," she says. "You have lessons, you have to pay for uniforms, you have to be dedicated."

Also like any other sport or activity, pageantry requires that competitors learn skills from trained coaches. Vaughan, Kennedy says, "definitely has the skills that are required for someone who I want my daughter to spend time with."

Elizabeth hadn't competed in pageants before she began working with Vaughan. As Elizabeth practices her "Rocker" routine with Vaughan, mom Cristina Hinds says that the most important thing about Elizabeth's new hobby is that she enjoys it.

But, beyond that, Hinds adds, Vaughan has "been able to bring out her personality. She always wins 'Best Personality,' and that's because Georgina has taught her how to express herself."

8

Beauty Pageants Celebrate Homogenity

Linda Wells

Linda Wells is editor-in-chief of Allure *magazine.*

It is sometimes difficult to tell pageant contestants apart without their identifying sashes, as they all are similar in appearance and reflect what American society generally believes to be beautiful. But pageants have become relics of the past, as it is now impossible to define what is beautiful in a single image. Beauty is being different; it is not looking like every other woman.

I used to watch beauty pageants as if they would change the course of history. I'd set up scorecards in front of the TV, make a bowl of popcorn, and drag the phone to the couch so my friend Penny and I could call each other and compare notes on talent versus swimsuit. My sister and I would root, hopelessly, for our home state at the time, knowing full well that Miss Connecticut didn't stand a chance against the slick and well-coached Misses Texas and California. It was sometimes hard to tell the contestants apart beyond their sashes— they were all flashy, glossy visions of what was generally believed to be American beauty.

A Relic of the Past

The beauty pageant in this country is a relic. At its peak in 1988, the television audience for the Miss America pageant was 33 million; by 2010, that number had fallen to 4.5 million. All anyone can remember about some of the recent pageant contestants are the scandals that surrounded them—the breast implants, the sex tapes, and the controversial opinions that fed morning news shows and late-night comedy for months afterward.

The pageant is an anachronism in every way, most essentially in what it presumes to celebrate. The notion of American beauty is impossible to contain in a single image today.

No Single Definition of Beauty

This is good news; there is no one definition of beauty. And even though people worry that plastic surgery and injections threaten to a create a new breed of uniform women, that is technically impossible, at least at the moment. Surgery conforms to the underlying bone structure for shape and contour. If anything, surgically altered bodies are alike only in their strangeness—a distortion of fish lips, pinched noses, frozen foreheads, and ballooning breasts. It's a subspecies made vivid on The Real Housewives of Fill-in-the-Blank.

Homogeneity is the enemy of beauty. There is no perfect nose, perfect skin tone, perfect body type, or perfect hair. The future of beauty lies in its variety. The human form is at its most seductive when it expresses individuality, not when it mirrors conformity. That's why the blonde-haired California surfer girl and the polished, busty pageant queen of the late twentieth century are such faded icons. A woman shouldn't have to declare her identity with a sash.

9

Some Beauty Pageants Let Women Embrace Who They Really Are

Laura Daniels

Laura Daniels was a student at the University of Gloucestershire in the United Kingdom when she wrote this viewpoint for the Huffington Post.

A beauty pageant in England is not just for tall, slim, young girls, but for plus-size women who celebrate their large sizes. This pageant allows women to embrace who they are and show that every woman is different and perfect in her own way.

You flick through the TV channels, where you stop on a television programme, which follows the lives of four beauty pageant models. What do you expect to see? Tall, slim, tanned young girls, how wrong you are.

This isn't any normal beauty pageant; of course, you'll have the normal sparkly over the top dresses, the embellishment of various body parts and the smallest, tightest bikini tops you can imagine. This beauty pageant has a twist; these models are sized 18 plus.

The Big Beautiful Woman Pageant

Welcome to the Big Beautiful Woman Pageant, the competition where Britain's most stunning plus sized models celebrate their beauty without feeling an ounce of guilt in doing-so. I have to be honest; there aren't many larger women I know who celebrate the idea. After all, being called overweight, or even obese, isn't something many women set out to achieve.

For starters, is this not making a mockery of the government's healthy Body Mass Index campaign? I mean, in the past I've faced numerous ear bashings from the nurse, where she delightfully told me I was overweight and ought to do something about it. After all, it cuts years off my life. If you've been fortunate to escape the boundary complying nurse then I'm sure you've come into contact with the 'Change Your Life' advertisements. It's enough to make you feel temporarily guilty, until you reach for the chocolate bar anyway.

Self-indulgence is celebrated in this contest, as is being unhealthy and being obese. There is no limit to this competition, apart from the fact you have to be a size 18, at least. Horrifyingly, you could weigh 50 tons and be greeted with open arms into the competition.

A Feeling of Confidence

The documentary, features four young girls who are on a quest to win the Big Beautiful Woman Pageant. I'm sure you are all thinking, what's the incentive for competing, with the word 'money' springing to mind. This isn't the case, the one and only prize these girls win is a sash declaring their temporary title—Mrs. B.B.W International. Perhaps the most important prize comes from within, the feeling of happiness and confidence—which can often be left quashed by the public's perceptions of larger women.

I'm sure many people, particularly women, will shriek in horror as they witness the models strutting their stuff nearly nude in a bikini down a catwalk. It isn't the weight, size or amount of cellulite that worries me about these women; instead it is the emotional instability that could occur due to them exposing themselves, physically and emotionally to a mass audience. Confidence is something these girls ooze in front of the camera, but humans are complex creatures. Who isn't to say they are feeling vulnerable and ashamed. After all, they each have their own reason for applying to the pageant and it isn't just to win a tiara.

These ladies are embracing their lives, and why shouldn't they?

Women's magazines relentlessly dictate to the nation the perfect size, shape and weight of the most stunning celebrities, people who are role models to women internationally. Regardless of who you are, if you do not fit into this 'perfect' criterion, then you can feel disappointed and unworthy of any attention. After all, we can all achieve the perfect photo shopped figure that appears on the front of every magazine, can't we?

Embracing Who They Are

Everyday women are left feeling like they are failures because they don't have the perfect hourglass figure complete with the 20-inch waist. Instead, they are flawed with cellulite, dimples and stretch marks. While it's easy to become infatuated with our flaws, they represent who we are. And, while this pageant may not be everyone's ideal, who are we to fault them for embracing who they are?

Often larger women are left ostracized from society based purely on their size; if an individual did this to someone based on their disability there would be a national outcry. These ladies are embracing their lives, and why shouldn't they? They aren't trying to change the national average size of women, they are just showing that everyone is different, and everyone is perfect in their own way. What is so wrong with girls being obese and happy? I see plenty of skinny size 6's who look completely miserable.

In all honesty, I can't hate this pageant even if the thought of myself being a size 18 (something I got very close to in the past) does leave me quivering inside. This documentary promotes living your life. As someone who has spent the last two years of my life dieting, this leaves me feeling uplifted. Why worry about being skinny, when we can be skeletons once our life has finished. You may as well just live for the moment and be a better person on the inside.

10

Not Irony: Beauty Pageants Make Strong Women

Sabrina Nooruddin

Sabrina Nooruddin has placed in and won several beauty pageants; she was a student at the University of Georgia at the time of this writing.

Women who compete in pageants must be poised, confident, and articulate, traits that transfer well to real-life situations. In addition, pageant competitions teach contestants stage presence and grace, how to meet new people, and how to interview and speak effectively. Most pageants are more than judging someone on her beauty, and in fact are moving away from beauty only to emphasize other aspects of the individual.

Do you remember the feeling of seeing a rectangle box under the Christmas tree? That tall beautiful medley of cardboard and plastic could only mean one thing: a new Barbie doll. After 25 minutes and a combination of scissors, tweezers, hands, and teeth, there I sat: a seven-year-old Indian-American girl stoking her beautiful blonde hair and I remember thinking to myself that she was *perfect.*

My entire life I was convinced that the perfect woman looked exactly like Barbie, and I had every reason to believe so. The actresses on television, models on the runways, and beauty queens in Miss America were just that: tall, blonde, and skinny, and that's where it hit me: by only crowning a certain "Barbie-like" image we as a society are deeming that others outside of that very small population are inferior in terms of beauty. So I made it my mission, to become part of the solution, and start with the problem.

Service is where I come from and it is where I intend to go. My dream is to work in a field with I can promote female empowerment and confidence in young women. My greatest intellectual endeavor could be my academic success in my short time during my undergraduate career, or intellectual can be defined as creative, something that made a difference in the lives of young women. My voluntary work with young girls throughout the community on public speaking, stage presence, and interview skills has encouraged me to develop my own program in conjunction with Girl Talk peer mentoring program. I collaborate with young female community leaders and titleholders to develop a mentoring program focused on diversity in middle school girls. These girls are paired with mentors to create a safe and secure place to discuss issues that affect them, like cyber bulling, Internet safety, communicating with parents, and self-image. I started working with teen girls at the Gwinnett Children's Shelter for all four years of high school where I conducted Girl's Groups, interactive activities that engage the residents and encourage them to talk about their issues that affect them and communicate with other residents. I truly believe that peer to peer mentoring is the best way to reach out to community residents and help them to do things they didn't think were possible and realize all of the doors that are open to us.

"Beauty Without Barriers"

I got involved with pageantry two years ago and have participated in four pageants since. With three titles to my name I have made it my mission to speak out about my platform and talk to young girls about what it really means to be "beautiful." I understand the irony in promoting "Beauty Without Barriers" in a *beauty* pageant, but the pageants that I participate in and coach other young women for are scholarship organizations that require women to be poised, elegant, talented, and well-spoken. I have personally seen the difference pageants can make in a young woman's self-confidence and her ability to present herself in interviews and in front of large audiences.

With talent, interview, platforms, and question-answer segments, pageants are moving away from aesthetics and forcing contestants to be well-spoken, knowledgeable, and graceful young ladies.

While *Toddlers and Tiaras* is still infecting televisions all over the world, pageant girls are fighting to keep the reputation of pageantry positive. I have always loved to get dressed up and was born with competitive bones in my body, but my mother was against pageants from the start. On my nineteenth birthday, the only thing I asked for was support in the Miss India Georgia pageant that summer. My mother bit her tongue the entire summer, although occasionally I heard a "waste of time" under her breath. However, come show time my mom stood by my side through hair, makeup, and dressed me for quick changes. I could not have done it without her and the moment they called my name I looked directly at her and saw a tear run down her face. Even my own mother, the ultimate pageant skeptic, is a true believer in the confidence and character that pageantry builds.

Hidden Benefits of Pageants

Months later I interviewed for summer internships and was lucky enough to get two amazing offers, both complimenting me on my excellent interview skills. I credit much of my quick thinking and ability to express myself to pageants. Additionally, other hidden benefits of competing in are poise and the ability to command attention when speaking. When I work as a coach the first thing I do is make sure that my girls set a goal for themselves, and "winning" is not an option. The girls must focus on other benefits of pageantry like stage presence, meeting new people, improving interview skills, poise & grace, etc.

I will not deny that some pageants are nothing more than a group of outsiders judging someone on their physical beauty, but most pageants are much more than just that. With talent, interview, platforms, and question-answer segments, pageants are moving away from aesthetics and forcing contestants to be well-spoken, knowledgeable, and graceful young ladies who are passionate about a purpose.

Last June [2010], I competed in a pageant that was specifically designed for women under 5'5 tall thus giving an equal opportunity for young women to become role models and promote their platforms. I was crowned the first ever Miss USA Petite and given the ability to speak out against the phenomenon of "beauty."

Even with my seven inch crown, I still bear no resemblance to Barbie, but I do have the platform and the opportunity to speak to young women about what it really means to be "beautiful" and comfortable in your own skin. "Beauty without Barriers" is a program I have successful begun to develop with the help of other successful young women. The peer mentoring group pairs local, state, and national beauty queens with middle school girls to talk about important issues like body image, bullying, and cyber safety. My goal is to promote female empowerment at the young age and help young girls feel comfortable and "beautiful" no matter what shape, size, or color they are.

11

Beauty Pageants Make Women Feel Beautiful

Lingbo Li

While a student at Harvard University, Lingbo Li participated in the Miss USA pageant in 2010 and wrote about her experiences in her blog, Lingboli.com.

Women enter beauty pageants for different reasons, and the contestants have varying levels of pageant experience. Preparing for a beauty pageant is stressful and demanding: contestants must diet, work out regularly, purchase the right accessories, and prepare for the interview questions. Despite the emphasis on beauty, the contestants have many other excellent qualities other than their looks, and the diversity of the physical appearance of each was surprising. A beauty pageant is an opportunity for a woman to wear a pretty dress and feel beautiful, which isn't a bad thing.

04 OCTOBER 2010
WHY I'M ENTERING A BEAUTY PAGEANT

I watched Miss America as a child. I was 8, maybe 9. I remember Miss Hawaii won Miss Congeniality, but I forget who took the crown. What I remember even more clearly was the lone Asian contestant vying for the national title. She seemed a little softer than the other contestants, a little less sexily taut, and I was torn between rooting for her based on our ethnic similarities or emotionally selling out to support the blondes who I wish I could be.

Now I'm 20. I got into Harvard with my well-rounded-ness—when I used to report on admissions for the *The Harvard Crimson*, Dean of Admissions Bill Fitzsimmons looked up my file and told me offhand, "Yep, you were one of the all-arounders." I tried to do everything. I did some human rights stuff, I edited the school newspaper, I freelanced for a local paper, and dutifully attended karate twice a week.

But deep down, really, I always wondered what it would be like to be both beautiful and stupid; to do nothing but focus on your appearance rather than brains. I thought it'd be kind of glorious, an easy existence, even with evidence to the contrary. Now, I wonder more about how my ethnic background, which doesn't reach too much farther than skin tone and bone structure, will affect my career aspirations. Will anyone—and by anyone, I mean the bulk of Caucasian America—be able to relate to me?

Why I Entered a Beauty Pageant

This is all a long way of saying that part of the reason why I find entering Miss New York USA (part of Donald Trump's Miss USA circuit, not the Miss America pageant) an interesting experience is because it is truly something that the 8-year-old in me finds thrilling, a little subversive, obviously ludicrous. I was inspired to apply since 2009's title holder is Tracey Chang, who was also born in China, although she left at a much later age than I did. And while part of me is entering just "for the experience"—which is the only reason to do anything—part of me also wonders if I would be qualified to represent this country, or some part of this country.

I know that while I could drum up a convincing-sounding argument in my favor, that plenty of people would disagree.

This may be a country of immigrants, but some immigrants seem more American than others.

Part of why I'm entering is superficial: it's to get in shape and have an excuse to take care of myself. I'm drinking my 8 glasses of water a day, cutting out coffee, and trying to get as much sleep and exercise as I can fit in. My skin looks much better, my head feels clearer, and though I still have a few pounds to shed, it seems being healthy is a worthwhile endeavor, all the better if there's a goal in mind. It's tough, though. Loving food is not necessarily bad for staying in shape—there are many ways to love food—but moderation is tough!

An Undercover Mission

On Thanksgiving weekend, I'll be competing and living out the third reason why I'm doing this—as an undercover mission. What's the beauty pageant world like? What are the girls like? How many surgical enhancements might I spot? Will this ruin my self-esteem? Will I be able to glide in 4.5 inch gold stilettoes? How much tape will I need to adhere my bikini to my body? Will I feel totally ridiculous?

What doesn't kill me, I hope, will just make me stronger. And more sparkly. . . .

22 NOVEMBER 2010

DUDE, I'M SO STRESSED.

It's really, really hard to be beautiful.

Prepping for a beauty pageant is probably one of the most stressful, physically, and psychically demanding things I've done.

Let's ignore so-called "natural beauty" for a second as a freakish genetic aberration—which it is—since the confluence of genes and cultural values is not something any of us can control.

There are many kinds of beauty, and I'd argue that the beauty queen type of beauty is a pretty inhospitable one, an exaggerated, gay man's ideal of womanhood. Different pageants also [have] different ideals of beauty: Miss America doesn't really look like Miss USA, for example.

Pageants Are Stressful

The fact of the matter is, prepping for a beauty pageant is probably one of the most stressful, physically, and psychically demanding things I've done. Ok, so applying to college was more stressful, but it didn't require the workout schedule or dieting, just a welling up of anxiety. The mundane nature of beauty pageant stress centers around a few things:

- Am I tan enough?

- Am I tall enough?

- Am I skinny enough?

- Am I pretty enough?

- Do I need better shoes?

- Should I shell out another $200 for colored contacts?

- Do I need a new dress?

- OMG I CAN HAZ WORLD PEACE?!

Thinking about such really inconsequential things is pretty taxing. So what if you have a paper due? You haven't found the perfect pair of clear, 5 inch heels yet! (Just bought them, actually.) I have a sticky note on my computer with my chest-waist-hip measurements and approximate calorie counts of what I've eaten that day, along with reminders to myself in my inbox to buy superglue (broken earrings) and to go tanning. I still need a manicure. My heart tears up a bit every time I eat simple carbs. Etc.

I've been trying to do the two workouts a day routine, but this has proven pretty much impossible—I just don't have any energy left over. On the plus side, that despicable practice of tanning has proven to pretty fun and effective at optically slimming the body. There's just something about sitting a space pod bed of ultraviolet carcinogenic rays that is bizarrely calming and uplifting for the soul.

The first day of preliminaries is this Friday, so I only have to hold on for a few more days as I tie up loose ends. In the meantime, I'm exhausted! If you see me, feel free to give me a hug and give my stomach a poke—my abs have become a steel reserve. . . .

27 NOVEMBER 2010

MISS NEW YORK USA DAY

1: SWIMSUIT PRELIMINARY

I have been declared cattle contestant 247 in the Miss New York USA 2010 pageant.

Just Normal Girls

In all honesty, day 1 has been fun in the most wholesome of ways: all the girls (including myself) help each other behind the scenes. We cheer each other on. We compliment each other's swimsuits. We paint on obscene amounts of bronzer. We all have stretch marks, cellulite, big butts, flat hair, and un-gainly heels—and this makes everything ok. For some reason, I was expecting a room of Barbies, and there are a few Barbie-beautiful girls (who will win this pageant), but the majority of us are just you know, normal girls.

There are definitely varying levels of pageantry experi-ence—a former Miss New York Teen USA is competing for the Miss title, while another girl didn't bother to go tanning or buy a trendy swimsuit or make her hair enormous. I am satisfied that I'm somewhat prepared for this whole shebang.

My beautiful roommate was last year's 2nd runner up. We collapsed and munched on popcorn and pretzels after the swimsuit preliminary competition and watched The Sweetest Thing on TV.

This is all so happy and wholesome it is slightly ridiculous. If only Harvard were like, a giant slumber party with girls in bikinis and stripper heels. You know?

The schedule for tomorrow: interview (supposed to be really relaxed) around 10, lunch, evening gown rehearsal, then evening gown preliminary at 9pm. The actual pageant, and the announcement of the top 25, will be on Sunday. . . .

28 NOVEMBER 2010

BEHIND THE SCENES AT MISS NEW YORK USA, DAY 2

Welcome to another day of hair teasing, fake eyelashing, and uh, sitting around.

A lot of being in a pageant involves two activites:

Preparing and Waiting

1. Getting "ready"

- This takes at least two hours and 20 products and half a can of hairspray. Essential to the process is the tease-and-curl (not some crunk dance move) of backcombing strips of hair to create that 80's mall diva allure. I failed at this for evening gown.

2. Waiting

- You watch other contestants stomp/sashay/stumble down the carpeted runway whilst the MC herds you along like the incompetent 14 year olds you are. Sometimes this is punctuated with "spontaneous" Zumba lessons, which are CLEARLY scheduled in.

Yes kids, I eventually got up and shook my butt as well. I'm no pageant killjoy. I dance backstage before we get on as well . . . this was particularly true yesterday as we waiting in our bikinis and 6 inch heels to parade about like a particularly well-padded dog show.

The closing number included a former Miss Connecticut singing "Turn the Beat Around" while we all clapped and tried not to fall over in our interview suits.

The Interview

Speaking of the interview, it reminded me a lot of my speed dating experience, except it was speedier. We got two minutes with each judge. At least ten seconds was spent walking over and waiting for them to find our bio sheet. I accidentally frightened one by impatiently achievement-dumping him upon waiting for him to locate the bio sheet.

Me: So let me give you the short version. I'm a junior at Harvard and I've written internationally for publications and I helped found an NGO.

Him: Ok, take a deep breath.

Me: Ok.

Him: What do you do for fun?

Me: I like to eat out. I ate bull testicles! And calves brains! There was a video!!!

I'm not sure how that went.

I chilled out after that and fared much better. Sometime I got annoyed that a judge used our precious 30 seconds to talk about themselves . . . because there was so little time that there was almost no time to even give my "I'm awesome!!" elevator pitch.

(And by awesome, I mean dropping the H-Bomb shamelessly. I may not have the biggest hair, or uh, biggest other parts, but my education is really old, pretentious, and expensive!)

The Preliminaries

The evening gown preliminaries went off fine, except some GIRL stepped on my dressed and ripped a piece of the bottom. It was sewn up by a chaperone, thank god.

It's taken something as shallow and somewhat dehumanizing as a beauty pageant to realize that I have many other excellent qualities other than my physical appearance.

The key with evening gown is to walk very slowly and evenly, as if you're floating, and to radiate happiness and good will at the judges while keeping excellent posture.

I find out tomorrow during the final pageant whether I made it into the top 20 (possible!) or not. If I do, I'll compete in evening gown and swimsuit again. If I make it into the top five (doubtful!), I'd have to answer an on stage question taken from my bio sheet.

Dear blog readers, wish me luck on my journey towards breaking racial barriers. I'm just a humble Chinese-American girl chasing this red, white and blue dream. I'm an immigrant in a country built by immigrants. Boys barked at me in middle school—and it's haunted me ever since.

You know, it's funny that it's taken something as shallow and somewhat dehumanizing as a beauty pageant to realize that I have many other excellent qualities other than my physical appearance or ability to speed date a judge. Like my ability to purchase stylish evening wear for only $45! Second Time Around on Boston's Newbury St., baby....

30 NOVEMBER 2010

SOME REFLECTIONS ON PAGEANTRY

So it's back to being a civilian again.

I applied a slick of black eyeliner and donned my skinniest jeans to commemorate the thinnest that I have ever been—I'm doing some guilt-free gorging on sushi, Chinese food, and lattes for a few days.

A Lot to Be Thankful For

Being in a pageant made me realize (although my friends have been telling me for a long time) that I'm thin. For some reason, I assumed that every other contestant was going to be rail thin and super toned. Not so—the diversity of bodies on display was surprising, and I may not have been the leggiest or the blondest, but I realized after in the flesh, side by side comparison, that I should probably, you know, chill out. I have a lot be thankful for.

Thanks for all your support which is been so amazing—all the well wishes were much appreciated. I do wish, however, that I can avoid the look of disappointment on peoples' faces when I tell them I didn't place. I feel that I need to qualify not winning anything with a statement like, "Well, I messed up my interviews," or note that a lot of other contestants were convinced I'd make the top 20, and this feels like cheating what little insight I've gained from doing this. I wish that could more eloquently convey that brief hour or two of realization after not making the top 20 that I deserved to be up there without seeming self-righteous or a sore loser.

I'm beautiful the way I am! No, honestly, I am. I hadn't really believed it, but it finally seemed like the truth.

But losing is painful. I wonder how the other girls felt.

What fascinated me most were the girls there. While the girls in the top 20 were the kind I expected to find, the vast majority were far more interesting in their rationales of being there. A pageant, I realized, is really about the experience for some of them. It's an opportunity to wear a pretty dress, walk down a runway, have your photo taken, and feel like a queen for two minutes. It's a fantasy you buy.

But who am I to say that these girls don't deserve to spend their money and feel like they're beautiful too?

There was such a sadness to the fantasy. I came in convinced I couldn't win, realized that I was perfectly qualified to win, and left sad I didn't win anyway. Other girls seemed to come in not realizing the sharks they were up against. They wanted to believe they could be models, despite coming up many inches and pounds short. A lot of girls didn't understand what it meant to be in a pageant—that there were a certain kind of shoe you wore, a certain kind of dress you buy, an entire, fairly rigid series of rituals in preparing for competition.

These questions interested me a lot more, in the end, than what it meant to be Chinese in a non-racially defined pageant. However, it's worth noting that there was one other Asian girl there, who had won the New York title of the Miss Earth pageant, a cum laude grad from Penn with dancing awards under her belt. I felt like she was competition, and we never gravitated towards one another. She ended up making the top 20, but not going beyond that.

I'll post some more photos later, perhaps some more thoughts, but it's been an interesting—and utterly exhausting—journey. I'm glad to have met some fantastic people along the way, and I hope there's bigger and better stuff in store for me.

12

Transgender Contestants Should Be Allowed to Compete in Beauty Pageants

Emma Teitel

Emma Teitel is a columnist with Maclean's, *a Canadian weekly magazine.*

Beauty pageants are vapid and superficial, but nevertheless a transgendered woman should be allowed to compete with "natural born" women. If a transgendered woman looks like the other pageant contestants, then it is discrimination to keep her from competing. If a contestant is a woman now, then she should be allowed to compete.

There was a time, not so long ago, when Donald Trump demanded that Barack Obama surrender his birth certificate to the world to unequivocally prove his American citizenship. Now Trump, the co-sponsor of the Miss Universe pageant along with NBC, is being prevailed upon to produce a credential of his own—call it his little apprentice—to prove his bona fides as a Mister. The woman asking to see the proof in question is Gloria Allred, the celebrity feminist lawyer representing the only transgendered contestant in this year's Miss Universe Canada competition: 23-year-old Jenna (nee Walter) Talackova of Vancouver. Last month Talackova was removed from the competition when organizers were informed that she failed to meet the "natural born woman" criterion in the pageant rulebook. Gloria Allred's response was swift and simple: if Talackova had to show "hers" to qualify for the pageant, the Donald, as competition sponsor, should have to show "his" in the spirit of fair play.

Online Petition Helped

Lucky for us, nobody showed anything. And Canadian law—which recognizes Talackova as an official female—melted Trump's icy heart (the same one that has coldly quashed entrepreneurial dreams on television for the past eight years) long enough for him to reinstate the 23-year-old into the competition. The law, that is, and possibly an online petition drafted by Change.org, the social activism website which recently brought you campaigns like "Let Ernie and Bert get married on Sesame Street," "Starbucks: stop using bugs to colour your strawberry-flavoured drinks," and the somewhat lesser-known Canadian campaign, "Canadian government: address the Aeronautics Act, which may ban trans people from flying."

If you can't even tell to begin with that she was once a he, why discriminate when you learn the truth?

"Miss Universe Canada, Donald Trump: reverse the unfair disqualification of Jenna Talackova!" was almost at its 45,000th signature when Talackova was allowed to re-enter the competition: a watershed moment for the trans community, according to activists. If she wins at the Canadian pageant, Talackova will accomplish another first (first transgendered Miss Universe Canada champion), and go on to represent her country on the world stage at the international Miss Universe competition in December.

The Right to Humiliate Oneself

Kudos to her. But can we please, for just a moment, take a more holistic look at this breed of spectacle, as it only happens every once in a while and we should savour it accordingly. It really doesn't get much richer than when human rights activists fight for the rights of minority groups to objectify, humiliate, and degrade themselves like everybody else. Or as the Toronto *Star's* editorialists put it, "could there be a more absurd place for a fight over dignity?" (In this case, a fight for the right to be undignified). It's only a matter of time before Change.org launches its "Let transgendered boys star in *Toddlers in Tiaras*" campaign. The Miss Universe Canada controversy is almost as painfully ironic as the Black Eyed Peas' African American frontman, Will.i.am, defending his right to don blackface at the 2010 MTV Video Music Awards.

It's also painfully dumb: The merits of Ms. Congeniality notwithstanding, pageants are vapid and superficial; their beauty is skin deep. So why should Talackova's go any deeper? In other words, if she looks the part, what else matters? It's called a beauty pageant for a reason. As Robyn Urback argued cannily in the National Post, Talackova looks just like her pageant counterparts—most of whom have probably had as many lip injections as she's had hormonal ones. So a note to future Miss Universe organizers: if you can't even tell to begin with that she was once a he, why discriminate when you learn the truth?

Transgenders Are Now Equal

In the end, thanks to Canadian law—and Donald Trump's choice to respect it—Talackova will no longer face discrimination in her fight for the right to be objectified; nor will every trans woman and child after her. And it's very possible that her supposed handicap could transform into a legitimate advantage. After all, what's more impressive? A beautiful bikini-clad woman, or a beautiful bikini-clad woman who used to be a man? There's no denying that Talackova will get an A for effort where her opponents won't even qualify. And with transphobia on its way out—however slowly that exit may occur—chances are audiences will be increasingly impressed with, rather than put off by, a beautiful transgendered contestant. Who knows? One day it might be the "naturally born" females hiring the likes of Gloria Allred and crying foul play. Stranger things have happened. So perhaps where one Miss Universe rule was discarded, another should be added: if you're a woman now, you were always a woman—at least in the eyes of the judges. A Change.org petition signatory wrote online recently, "Her being trans represents that it was harder for her than most to get where she is today, and that makes her the perfect Miss Universe contestant." Not so. Jenna Talackova is no more or less qualified than any of her fellow competitors. She is merely equal to them. And that is her triumph.

13

Transgenders Should Not Be Allowed to Compete in Beauty Pageants

Jesse Kline

Jesse Kline has written for many publications, including the National Post, Reason, *and the* Western Standard.

Although a transgendered woman may look like a woman, and she may feel like she is a woman, she was not always a woman. Beauty pageants have the right to set their own rules, and it is a reasonable requirement that the contestants be born female. An inclusive society should treat all people, including transgenders, with respect and dignity, but it does not mean that transgenders must be allowed to compete in beauty pageants.

Jenna Talackova seemed to have everything going for her and had high hopes of competing in the Miss Universe Canada beauty pageant in May. She was one of 65 finalists who was chosen to take part. Only problem is that this beautiful young woman hasn't always been, well, a woman.

After claiming to have identified herself as a female, despite being born male, at a very young age, Ms. Talackova began hormone therapy as a teenager and underwent a sex reassignment surgery two years ago.

A statement from Miss Universe Canada said that Ms. Talackova was disqualified because "she did not meet the requirements to compete despite having stated otherwise on her entry form." Although the event organizers have not said that she was disqualified for being born a man, it certainly looks that way. On first blush, this seems like a case of discrimination—if the most beautiful woman happens to have been born a man, why should she not be able to compete against other women?

Even if Ms. Talackova may have always *felt* she was a woman, the fact is that she wasn't. It's not unreasonable to say that contestants should be natural females in order to compete. That's not to say we shouldn't have transgendered beauty contests—in fact, a simple Google search reveals they already exist. Perhaps we should have one that is distinctly Canadian. If there are enough people who want to compete in such an event and enough people who want to watch it, then someone will surely start one. That is the beauty of living in a free society.

Organizations Should Be Able to Set Their Own Rules

But living in a free society also means allowing private organizations the right to set the rules of their competitions as they see fit. If the organizers of the Miss Universe Canada pageant want only natural-born females to enter, that is their right. And in this case, the decision makes sense. It makes sense from a business perspective—the Miss Universe pageant clearly doesn't want to meddle with any controversial social issues, and it makes sense bio ethically: With the increased availability of sex-change operations and the ability to genetically enhance people potentially not far off, this issue is not going away any time soon. Much like in sport, people should be allowed to compete based on their *natural* abilities.

We should all be working towards a more inclusive society, but being inclusive also means allowing people and organizations to set their own rules. Ms. Talackova has the right to live her life with full equality under the law and should be treated with respect and dignity by all, but no one has the right to qualify in whatever beauty pageant they please. Suggesting otherwise is not only unfair to the organizers and sponsors of the Miss Universe pageant, but further waters down the meaning of what true discrimination really means.

14

Transgender Beauty Pageants Are a Sign of Progress

Kate Linthicum

Kate Linthicum is a writer for the Los Angeles Times.

A beauty contest for transgender women is a way for the contestants to express their femininity. The women's movement has allowed women to enter many professions and activities that had been previously closed to them due to their gender. But in the process, many women feel they have to hide their femininity in order to compete with men in school and in the workplace. Competing in a beauty pageant is just one way for women to express their womanhood, and now that opportunity is open to transgender women as well.

A little before noon last Sunday, I pulled up outside a nightclub in Hollywood.

I had come to check out rehearsals for a beauty pageant being staged that night at Circus Disco, a kitschy bar tucked back from the street on an unglamorous stretch of Santa Monica Boulevard. The idea of ranking women on their looks had always seemed objectionable, like a step backward from feminism. But this pageant sounded special. The Queen USA contest is billed as "the premier transgender beauty pageant in the United States."

Past a portico topped with a statue of a dancing tiger, a side door led into a cavernous dance hall. A flock of women in workout clothes and heels were moving in formation. "Hips, hips, hips, hips!" a choreographer yelled. "I know it's lunch time, but I want to see some energy!"

As the routine took shape, a slim woman with long blond hair looked on approvingly. Karina Samala is the reigning "Empress" of the Imperial Court of Los Angeles and Hollywood, the lesbian, gay, bisexual and transgender advocacy group that puts on the pageant every year. Samala was born a boy in the Philippines, but says she always felt like a girl inside. As a kid, she used to sneak into her sisters' dresses.

A Double Life

After immigrating to the United States in her 20s, she found a community of people like her at the drag clubs of West Hollywood, where she would do impersonations on stage (she was best as Cher).

"But I was trying to live a double life," she said. "I had to go to work in a suit and tie and at night I would go back to being Karina, performing in gay bars."

Samala began her medical transition to becoming a woman a decade ago, around the time she retired from her job as a senior engineer at Northrop Grumman.

She's now involved with half a dozen advocacy groups and advisory boards, including one that helped establish transgender-only cells in Los Angeles city jails earlier this year. She's trying to implement similar changes at Los Angeles County jails, and is also working with a nonprofit to create a free medical clinic to meet the specific health needs of transgender women.

When she's not shuttling between meetings, Samala is checking in with the dozens of young people around Los Angeles who call her a mentor, or simply "Mother Karina."

Confidence and Self-Esteem

She pushes them to compete in pageants, which she says helps boost the confidence of a population that doesn't often get a lot of support.

Samala knows what winning a pageant can do for self-esteem. She is a former Queen Universe. The pageant was about to begin. In the dressing room backstage, it felt like prom night. Contestant Bramyla Wilson, looking glamorous with thick curls and a sparkly red dress, was still mulling which heels to wear.

"The silver ones?" Wilson asked.

"The silver ones," her friend, Kimora Belisle, agreed.

Few women who are born women feel they can be "overtly feminine" these days because they're expected to compete with men in school and in the workplace.

Wilson moved here from Alabama a few years ago. When I asked her how the transgender community in L.A. compares to the one back home, she looked at me like I was crazy. "There is no community in Alabama," she said.

Before taking the stage, Wilson clasped hands with her rivals in a circle. Each was at a different stage of their transition. Some had had plastic surgery, others had not. Many were immigrants, from Asia or Latin America.

"By the grace of God we are still here," Wilson prayed. "We are still standing strong."

Then they strutted on stage. The crowd went wild as they flipped their hair, pursed their lips and batted their eyelashes. A panel of judges—including a plastic surgeon and two West Hollywood city councilmen—took note.

"They put some women to shame," a man in the crowd said to me during the swimsuit competition.

I was taken aback.

Sure, the women on stage were good. Some were Miss America good, and had the cliched gestures of femininity down pat.

Is There More to Being a Woman?

But isn't there more to being a woman?

Backstage, Juliana Giessel was celebrating her win in the swimsuit contest. During opening introductions onstage, she had pumped a fist in the air and declared, "I am a woman!" Giessel said few women who are born women feel they can be "overtly feminine" these days because they're expected to compete with men in school and in the workplace.

In simpler terms, she was saying feminism killed femininity.

But that misses the point.

More Opportunities

What the women's movement has done is open up opportunities. Just look at Carmen Hinayon, who won the Queen USA crown in 2009. This fall, Hinayon will start at UCLA law school so she can take her fight for lesbian, gay, bisexual and transgender rights to the courts.

Fifty years ago, law school was rare for any woman, transgender or not.

There are countless expressions of womanhood now, from female Olympic gymnasts to women cops to moms who decide to stay home with their kids.

And those who choose to compete in beauty pageants, Queen USA included—well, that's an authentic expression, too.

But are we ready to accept them for who they are?

Later that night, during a question-and-answer session, the contestants ticked off harrowing incidents of violence and discrimination they have faced simply for being themselves.

"We are existing," one contestant said.

"We will be a part of your world whether you like it or not," vowed another.

Beyond the flashy lashes and shiny lips, strength and determination shone through. And it was clear that those are qualities of womanhood, too.

15

All Women, Even Transgenders, Should Give Up Beauty Pageants

Suzi Parker

Suzi Parker is an Arkansas-based political and cultural journalist.

Allowing transgendered women to enter beauty pageants is good for equal rights, but ideally no women should participate in beauty pageants. Pageants try to make women fit into one mold of what is considered beautiful, and that ideal is decided by a panel of judges. Transgendered women should say that now that they have the right to compete in pageants, they do not want it. Being a woman is not just about having the right body shape, perfectly styled hair, and glossy lipstick.

The Miss Universe beauty pageant will now allow transgender women to strut their stuff for a crown. But maybe they should think twice about wanting to do so.

The Miss Universe organization, owned by Donald Trump, initially disqualified Canadian Jenna Talackova, 23, because she is a transgender woman. But now the pageant has consulted with the Gay and Lesbian Alliance Against Defamation (GLAAD) to change its policy from only allowing "naturally born" women.

Gay rights groups are heralding the change as a win similar to when the Olympics and the Girl Scouts of America first allowed transgender people to participate in their organizations. It is a good day for equal rights, but why would any woman—transgender or otherwise—want a pageant queen life?

Living Up to a Beauty Ideal

Go ahead, call me a feminist. The real victory would be if no women desired pageant queen status. Now, transgender women will have to be like the rest of us—living up to a beauty ideal decided by a panel of judges.

When I was six years old, my mom entered me in a pageant. I wore a hooped white Southern belle dress and curls—a miniature version of Vivian Leigh in "Gone With The Wind." The pageant, held in the ballroom at a local hotel, was small, a preliminary to something bigger. It seemed natural to strut across the stage—after all, I took dance lessons.

I didn't win. Afterwards, my father informed my mother that I would no longer be a pageant girl. Ever the eagle eye, he had seen a woman pay off a judge. Her daughter won.

Jaded at an early age, I watched my friends doll up for pageants over the years. They spent thousands on dresses and added plastic surgery to their pageant costs. They tanned and they worried about their weight. It was ridiculous.

The Miss Universe pageant is an international competition with more than 75 countries represented. Contestants must be between the ages of 18 and 27. Unlike the Miss America pageant, the Miss Universe pageant doesn't require a talent but rather focuses on swimsuit and evening gown competitions with finalists answering an impromptu live question.

Serving as an Advocate

Talackova told ABC News' Barbara Walters, "I feel like the universe, the creator just put me in this position as an advocate. And now it's like this, and I'll take that position. If it's helping anybody else, my story and my actions, then I feel great about it."

Changing rules and breaking barriers don't always crack the glass ceiling.

Just ask Talackova's lawyer, Gloria Allred. She's in a flame-throwing verbal match against Trump. [In April 2012], before Talackova was allowed into the pageant, Allred said, "She did not ask Mr. Trump to prove that he is a naturally born man or to see photos of his birth to view his anatomy to prove that he was male."

Trump tweeted a nasty—and sexist—message to Allred.

"I made my decision to allow Jenna Talackova to partici-pate in Miss Universe Canada two days before Gloria Allred got involved," he tweeted. "I hope Jenna is not paying Gloria a fee other than all the free publicity that Gloria is getting for no reason. Is Gloria a man or a woman????—few men would know the answer to that one."

What Is a Woman?

Talackova, who said she was often bullied as a teenager, could make a stand for women.

She could defend Allred. She could say that now that she has the chance to be a beauty queen, she doesn't want it. She could tell Trump to cram his pageant.

It would be refreshing if she told the world that being a woman isn't just about curves in the right places, glossy lip-stick and perfectly coiffed hair. Womanhood—and the dis-crimination that comes with God-given assets or medically created ones—is so much more than sparkly pageant gowns.

But sadly, the pageant bug—and its trappings—have likely bit her.

16

The Miss USA Beauty Pageant Was Rigged

Sheena Monnin, as told to Ann Curry

Sheena Monnin was Miss Pennsylvania USA and competed in the Miss USA pageant in 2012. She alleged that the final five contestants were already selected before the final sixteen were announced. She resigned in protest at the conclusion of the pageant. Ann Curry was an anchor with the morning television show Today.

The results of the Miss USA beauty pageant were written in a list that was seen by a Miss USA participant before the final sixteen contestants were announced. Choosing the final five contestants before the final sixteen is an injustice to all the participants in all the Miss USA pageants. It is also fraudulent.

[Editor's note: Sheena Monnin resigned as Miss Pennsylvania USA immediately following the 2012 Miss USA pageant, saying that the results had been predetermined. Monnin claimed that Miss Florida, Karina Brez, had told her she had seen a list of the five finalists before the top sixteen contestants had been announced.]

*A*nn Curry: Sheena Monnin is now joining us for her first interview since resigning as Miss PA USA. Sheena, good morning.

Sheena Monnin: Good morning, thank you.

Your reaction to the latest from Donald Trump that he is now speaking about suing you.

Yes, I feel disappointed that he has made some of the statements that he's said about me. And I feel prepared to continue to pursue the truth. I know what I heard, and I know what I in turn witnessed come true, based on what I heard the contestant [say] she saw the list. So I'm prepared to continue to march forward. And what I really want out of this is for the truth to be known. I want to make sure that I stand out for what I believe is right. I know what I heard, there's no doubt in my mind that the contestant was serious, when she laid out what she said she saw. I believe her to be true.

You're talking about Miss Florida [Karina Brez].

I am.

She had just seen something that would potentially, drastically change the reputation of the Miss Universe Organization. And this is a big deal.

The pageant revealed had said something about a list. Now we just heard in this report that she's saying it was a joke. And that the winner was not even on this list. Is it possible you misinterpreted what she said?

Absolutely not.

Why are you so sure?

I have many years of psychological training. I know when someone is telling a joke, I know when someone is scared, and when someone is serious. And in my opinion, her body language was very serious and she looked a little bit scared because she had just seen something that would potentially, drastically change the reputation of the Miss Universe Organization. And this is a big deal.

So what happened then? I want you to clarify. You're saying that she came to you in a very serious way and said that there was a list of five names.

Yes.

And how did she say that to you? And what was your reaction?

Yes, after the top 16 were called and we were back stage she said that she had seen a list with the names of the top five. And I said, "Well, who do, who do you think the top five are going to be?" And she said, "I know who the top five are going to be because I saw this list." And my reaction was, well let's wait and see who the top five really are, because maybe that was a rehearsal list. I mean, there are many reasons that a list could be laying around with the top five names, but when the names were called out in the order that she said she saw them on the list, that's just too coincidental to not be true.

You had a very strong reaction when those names were called out.

I did. Yes. And I still feel that strong reaction. Because I feel that an injustice has been done. Not only to the other people who were not in the top five, but to the thousands of pageant girls across the nation who compete believing this is an honest system, as I did for nine years, believing this is an honest system.

You've just heard that pageant officials are saying your real reason for resigning is that you disagree with a new policy to admit transgender contestants.

Yes.

Is this possible? Is this true? Does that have any part of your decision?

There are a myriad of reasons why I'm resigning. That is an issue that I discussed with my state director back in April. And his reaction was, "Sheena, why don't you formulate an answer so if you're asked in an interview or on stage you can state your opinion in a public way?" And I thought that was fair. So I continued to serve the title, and I continued to prepare for Miss USA. But later on, in my initial statement, I also mentioned fair play. I did not elaborate on that when I initially emailed my state director because I didn't see the list. If I would have seen the list I would have reacted in a very strong, matter-of-fact way. So I didn't feel since I didn't see the list, that that was a valid reason at that time for resignation. . . .

There's just too, too much evidence pointing to this being fraudulent.

If you didn't see the list, you didn't see the list, so then how do you know the pageant is rigged?

I think it's too coincidental, for someone to be able to call out in order the top five before the top 16 were even narrowed down. To me, that just doesn't make sense, that's not logical, that that could actually be.

You seem very calm in the face of what appears to be a lawsuit coming your way from Donald Trump. Do you have a message for him this morning?

My message is very simple. I would like the truth to be made known. I am not here to destroy anyone. I am not here to bad talk about anybody. My heart and my attitude is, I want the truth to be made known. And in my opinion, what Miss Florida said is true, there's really no doubt in my mind. There's just too, too much evidence pointing to this being fraudulent.

And you say you have actually received some sort of mediation effort.

I have received some, some legal documentation, yes, giving me options for the future. I'm not sure yet which options I will take, but I do know that moving forward, my main motivation will remain the same.

Sheena Monnin, thank you for joining us.

Thank you.

Organizations to Contact

The editors have compiled the following list of organizations concerned with the issues debated in this book. The descriptions are derived from materials provided by the organizations. All have publications or information available for interested readers. The list was compiled on the date of publication of the present volume; the information provided here may change. Be aware that many organizations take several weeks or longer to respond to inquiries, so allow as much time as possible.

A Minor Consideration
15003 S. Denker Ave., Gardena, CA   90247
e-mail: ppetersen@msn.com
website: www.minorcon.org

A Minor Consideration is a nonprofit foundation formed to give guidance and support to child performers, including child beauty pageant participants. The foundation works to provide a strong emphasis on education and character development, plus helps to preserve the money these children generate. The foundation offers many articles on its website, including original editorials on the topic of child performers and beauty pageants.

Concerned Women for America (CWA)
1015 Fifteenth St. NW, Suite 1100, Washington, DC   20005
(202) 488-7000 • fax: (202) 488-0806
e-mail: mail@cwfa.org
website: www.cwfa.org

Concerned Women for America (CWA) is a public policy women's organization that seeks to bring Biblical principles into all levels of public policy. The Beverly LaHaye Institute of the CWA focuses on family issues, feminist and women's issues, and social and cultural concerns. Among the resources on the organization's website is the commentary "Size 16 Model Contends for Beauty Title."

Feminist Majority Foundation (FMF)
1600 Wilson Blvd., Suite 801, Arlington, VA   22209
(703) 522-2214 • fax: (703) 522-2219
e-mail: media@feminist.org
website: www.feminist.org

The Feminist Majority Foundation (FMF), which was founded in 1987, is an organization dedicated to women's equality, reproductive health, and nonviolence. FMF engages in research and public policy development, public education programs, grassroots organizing projects, leadership training and development programs, and participates in and organizes forums on issues of women's equality and empowerment. A variety of literature, including some that mention beauty pageants, is available on its website, as well as links to other resources such as feminist magazines.

Miss America Organization
222 New Rd., Suite 700, Linwood, NJ   08221
(609) 653-8700 • fax: (609) 653-8740
e-mail: info@missamerica.org
website: www.missamerica.org

The Miss America Organization runs the Miss America pageant. The Miss America program provides personal and professional opportunities for young women to promote their voices in culture, politics, and the community. Available on its website is information about the competition, including key facts and figures about the history of the Miss America pageant, first held in 1921.

Miss Universe Organization
1370 Avenue of the Americas, 16th Floor
New York, NY   10019
(212) 373-4999 • fax: (212) 843-9200
website: www.missuniverse.org

The Miss Universe Organization operates the Miss Teen USA, Miss USA, and Miss Universe pageants. Contestants in the Miss Universe pageants, which have crowned beauty queens for more than fifty years, compete with the hope of advancing their careers, promoting their personal and humanitarian goals, and improving the lives of others. Available on the Miss Universe Organization website is information about the organization and the three pageants it sponsors.

National Organization for Women (NOW)

1100 H St. NW, 3rd Floor, Washington, DC   20005
(202) 628-8NOW • fax: (202) 785-8576
website: www.now.org

The National Organization for Women (NOW) is a nonprofit organization devoted to furthering women's rights through education and litigation. For over a decade, NOW has led the Love Your Body campaign, which has the goal of countering the unrealistic beauty standards, gender stereotypes, and sometimes harmful images imposed by media advertisers on women. Available on NOW's website is information on the Love Your Body campaign, including information on staging a "mock beauty pageant."

Pull the Pin

e-mail: info@sayno4kids.com
website: www.pullthepin.com.au

Pull the Pin (on beauty pageants for children) began in Australia in response to the US beauty pageant company Universal Royalty announcing an Australian pageant. Pull the Pin believes that child beauty pageants send the wrong message to children, girls in particular. The organization contends that beauty pageants are exploitive and are not in the child's best interests. The organization would like to see an end to child beauty pageants by requiring all participants be at least sixteen years old, so that they can give informed consent to participating in pageants. Pull the Pin has campaigns in Australia, New Zealand, and the United States. Its website and Facebook pages have numerous articles about child beauty pageants.

Bibliography

Books

Susan Anderson   *High Glitz: The Extravagant World of Beauty Pageants*. Brooklyn, NY: PowerHouse Books, 2009.

Libba Bray   *Beauty Queens*. New York: Scholastic, 2011.

Hollie Domiano   *Myths America: A Practical Guide to Pageantry*. Charleston, SC: CreateSpace, 2010.

David Valdez Greenwood   *The Rhinestone Sisterhood: A Journey through Small-Town America, One Tiara at a Time*. New York: Crown, 2010.

Karen Kataline   *Fatlash! Food Police and the Fear of Thin—A Cautionary Tale*. Denver, CO: PRWeb, 2012.

Peggy Orenstein   *Cinderella Ate My Daughter*. New York: Harper, 2012.

Lu Parker   *Catching the Crown: The Source for Pageant Competition*, 2nd ed. Beverly Hills, CA: Parker Publications, 2008.

Susan Supernaw   *Muskogee Daughter: My Sojourn to the Miss America Pageant*. Lincoln: University of Nebraska Press, 2010.

Karen W. Tice   *Queens of Academe: Beauty Pageantry, Student Bodies, and College Life*. New York: Oxford University Press, 2012.

Vanessa Williams and Helen Williams — *You Have No Idea: A Famous Daughter, Her No-Nonsense Mother, and How They Survived Pageants, Hollywood, Love, Loss, and Each Other*. New York: Gotham, 2012.

Periodicals and Internet Sources

Jonica Bray — "Living Dolls," *Woman's Day (Australia)*, July 19, 2010.

Staceyann Chin — "Beauty and the Boob Tube," *The Advocate*, May 2009.

Laverne Cox — "The Right to Dream: Jenna Talackova's Miss Universe Slight," *Huffington Post*, March 30, 2012. www.huffingtonpost.com.

Anthony Daniels — "Differently, the Same: A Transsexual Beauty Queen and the Evolution of 'Tolerance,'" *National Review*, May 14, 2012.

Rosemary Ellis — "Pretty Babies," *Good Housekeeping*, August 2011.

Hilary Levey Friedman — "There She Goes: A Trailblazing, Feminist Beauty Queen," *Huffington Post*, March 15, 2011. www.huffingtonpost.com.

Nina Funnell — "Sugar and Spice: But All Things Nice?" *National Times (Australia)*, May 4, 2011.

Karen Ann Gajewski	"A Canadian Miss Universe Contestant Was Banned from the Pageant in March for Being Transgendered," *The Humanist*, May–June 2012.
Abigail Haworth	"No Mistresses Allowed," *Marie Claire*, August 2012.
Skip Hollandsworth	"Toddlers in Tiaras," *Good Housekeeping*, August 2011.
Don Kaplan	"TLC and Parents Are Exploiting Honey Boo Boo," *New York Daily News*, October 21, 2012.
Lauri Kubuitsile	"When a Winning Smile Is Not Enough," *New Internationalist*, April 2012.
Michael Mechanic	"Are Disney Princesses Evil?" *Mother Jones*, January–February 2011.
Henry Meller	"Meet the Real Eden Wood," *Woman's Day (Australia)*, August 1, 2010.
Jennifer Pollmiller	"All Hail the Queen," *American Cowboy*, December 2011.
Christine Rosen	"The Anti-Beauty Myth," *Commentary*, November 2010.
Linda Stasi	"End This Now!" *New York Post*, August 20, 2012.
Kate Sullivan	"Miss Representation," *Allure*, October 2011.

Michelle Tauber	"Much Ado About Boo Boo," *People*, September 10, 2012.
Charlotte Triggs	*"Toddlers & Tiaras* Controversy: Are They Growing Up Too Fast?" *People*, September 14, 2011.
Charlotte Triggs, Kay West, and Elaine Aradillas	"Toddlers & Tiaras: Too Much Too Soon?" *People*, September 26, 2011.
Amy Wallace	"Glamour Girls," *Los Angeles Magazine*, October 2009.
Molly Young	"Let No Man Despise Thy Youth," *New York*, July 11, 2011.

Index